Writing Effective User Stories

As a user,
I can express a business need
in User Story format
to get the IT solution I need

Thomas Hathaway
Angela Hathaway

Ordering Information:

Quantity sales. Special discounts are available on quantity purchases by
corporations, associations, and others. For details, contact the publisher at
books@BusinessAnalysisExperts.com.

The content of this book is also available as an eCourse at
http://businessanalysisexperts.com/product/video-course-writing-user-stories

ISBN: 1519100493
ISBN-978-1519100498

DEDICATION

This work is dedicated to future generations of Product Owners, Subject Matter Experts, Domain Experts, and anyone responsible for representing the business community's interests on an Information Technology project.

Thomas and Angela Hathaway

CONTENTS

ACKNOWLEDGMENTS

This publication would not have been possible without the active support and hard work of our daughter, Penelope Hathaway. We would also be remiss if we did not acknowledge the thousands of students with whom we have had the honor of working over the years. We can honestly say that every single one of you influenced us in no small way.

Finally, we would like to acknowledge Harvey, that fictional Pooka created by Mary Chase and made famous by the movie of the same name with James Stewart. Very early in our marriage we recognized that a third entity is created and lives whenever we work closely on a concept, a new idea, or a new product. Over the years, this entity became so powerful and important to us that we decided to name it Harvey and he should rightfully be listed as the author of this and all of our creative works. Unfortunately, Harvey remains an invisible being, living somewhere beyond our physical senses but real nonetheless. Without Harvey, neither this book nor any of our other publications would have been possible. For us, Harvey embodies the entity that any collaborative effort creates and he is at least as real as each of us. We would truly be lost without him.

PREFACE

User Stories are a great method for expressing stakeholder requirements, whether your projects follow an Agile, Iterative, or a Waterfall methodology. This book presents two common User Story structures to help you ensure that your User Stories have all the required components and that they express the true business need as succinctly as possible. It offers **5 simple rules** to ensure that your User Stories are the best that they can be. That, in turn, will reduce the amount of time needed in User Story elaboration and discussion with the development team.

After reading this book you will be able to:

- Translate business needs into well-structured User Stories
- Write User Stories that express the what and avoid the how
- Apply five simple rules for writing effective User Stories
- Clarify assumptions in User Stories by adding context
- Identify and remove ambiguous and subjective terms and phrases in User Stories
- Select the appropriate format for expressing User Stories for Agile Projects
- Write stakeholder requirements in User Story format that solve business problems
- Elaborate User Stories to identify measurable non-functional requirements

Meanwhile, please enjoy this Book. We appreciate any comments, suggestions, recommended improvements, or complaints that you care to share with us. You can reach us via email at:

Books@BusinessAnalysisExperts.com.

AUTHORS' NOTE

The term "User Story" is a relative new addition to our language and its definition is evolving. In today's parlance, a complete User Story has three primary components, namely the "Card", the "Conversation", and the "Criteria". Different roles are responsible for creating each component. The "Card" expresses a business need. A representative of the business community is responsible for expressing the business need. Historically (and for practical reasons) the "Card" is the User Story from the perspective of the business community. Since we wrote this book specifically to address that audience, we use the term "User Story" in that context throughout.

The "Conversation" is an ongoing discussion between a developer responsible for creating software that meets the business need and the domain expert(s) who defined it (e.g., the original author of the "Card"). The developer initiates the "Conversation" with the domain expert(s) to define the "Criteria" and any additional information the developer needs to create the application. There is much to be written about both the "Conversation" and the "Criteria", but neither component is dealt with in any detail in this publication.

A well-written User Story ("Card") can drastically reduce the time needed for the "Conversation". It reduces misinterpretations, misunderstandings, and false starts, thereby paving the way for faster delivery of working software. We chose to limit the content of this publication to the "User Story" as understood by the business community to keep the book focused and address the widest possible audience.

BUSINESS ANALYSIS USING USER STORIES

Questions answered in this chapter:

- What are User Stories?
- Where do they fit in an Agile or Waterfall methodology?

There are two fundamental roles in any business transaction, a customer (*one who wants or needs something*) and a provider (*one who has or can acquire that same thing*).

Bringing these two roles together has been a challenge mankind has faced since before civilization began. If the something in question is an Information Technology (IT) system, the terminology is more current but the basic challenge remains. Since we invented IT, the single biggest challenge has been communicating what the customer wants in a manner that the developers can deliver.

Online resources for you:

⇨ The Impact of Business Requirements on the Success of Technology Projects by Keith Ellis
http://www.batimes.com/articles/the-impact-of-business-requirements-on-the-success-of-technology-projects.html

⇨ CIO analysis: Why 37 percent of projects fail
http://www.zdnet.com/blog/projectfailures/cio-analysis-why-37-percent-of-projects-fail/12565

⇨ Why Do Projects Fail? *(different project studies)*
http://calleam.com/WTPF/?page_id=1445

⇨ View this chapter as a video for FREE
http://businessanalysisexperts.com/product/business-analysis-using-user-stories/

Until recently, "requirements" have been the answer. Requirements define the behaviors and qualities (a.k.a. functional and non-functional requirements) that the IT solution has to exhibit to meet the customer's need. How we express requirements at various levels of detail is a topic about which there is an on-going (and seemingly eternal) debate.

The IIBA® (International Institute of Business Analysis) has identified four distinct "levels" or "layers" of requirements, namely "Business, Stakeholder, Solution, and Transition" requirements that describe the solution in layers of detail.

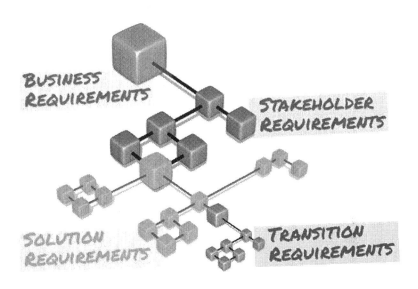

By this definition, "Business Requirements" are the basis upon which the organization initiates projects. The individual project then flushes out the detail in the remaining three levels.

Online resources for you:

⇨ What Are Requirements?
http://businessanalysisexperts.com/product/what-are-business-requirements-stakeholder-solution/

⇨ FREE Business Analysis Training
http://businessanalysisexperts.com/product-category/free-business-analysis-training/

⇨ Business Analysis Defined
http://businessanalysisexperts.com/product/video-course-business-analysis-defined/

Organizations using an Agile Software Development Methodology – aka SDM (in particular the SCRUM/XP flavors) propose replacing in particular the "Stakeholder" level with a concept called "User Stories".

Online resources for you:

⇨ Business Analysis and Agile Methodologies
http://businessanalysisexperts.com/product/business-analysis-agile-methodologies/

⇨ Backlog Refinement Meeting *(aka. Backlog Grooming)*
http://scrumtrainingseries.com/BacklogRefinementMeeting/BacklogRefinementMeeting.htm

---

But what, exactly, is a "User Story"?

In summary, a "User Story" is:

☑ Written from the perspective of a specific role the person initiating the interaction is playing

☑ A statement expressing the desired outcome of a single interaction with an IT system

☑ A mechanism for describing an IT system from the usage perspective

☑ Justified by the business objective or value the initiator is trying to achieve

☑ Replaces up-front documentation of "software requirements" with an ongoing dialog between users and developers

In current usage, a User Story describes a desired outcome from the perspective of a specified role or user type and explains the benefit.

Here are a few simple examples:

As a visitor (the role this individual plays when initiating this interaction), I can select the lowest fare flight that meets my travel needs (the outcome the role needs) to save money (the value the role receives).

Another example:

As a policyholder (role), I can see the account balances on all of my policies (outcome) to manage my financial obligations (value).

Both of these examples are "role-focused", meaning the role is identified first and the statement is written in the first person, namely "I". The goal or business value of the User Story is at the end. Recent discussions in the industry are moving toward changing the focus of this commonly recommended structure to focus on the value first and the role second. Following this paradigm, the examples would read:

To save money (the **value** the role receives), visitors (the **role** any individual plays when initiating this interaction) can select the lowest fare flight that meets my travel needs (the **outcome** the role needs).

and:

To manage financial obligations (**value**), policyholders (**role**) can see the account balances on all of their policies (**outcome**).

This structure removes the "I" focus and stresses the fact that there may be many people playing the role. Regardless of which structure you choose, you can see that each example is a statement (in each case, a single sentence) written from the usage perspective of a specific role.

Online resources for you:

⇨ Mr. Agile Talking About User Story Readiness
https://www.youtube.com/watch?v=rO3FSRC6xKY

⇨ New to User Stories? *(Written for the Scrum Alliance)*
https://www.scrumalliance.org/community/articles/2010/april/new-to-user-stories

From a developer perspective, I would need to know a whole lot more about what you are saying to be able to develop software to do it the way you want it, ergo, each example would require a dialog with the person in that role before I can start coding.

Notice that the role in each example is not a job title. The role-focused User Story forces the author of the story to focus on what they are trying to achieve in a very narrow context. Anyone can play the role, and in that role, need the same outcome for the same value. The goal-focused version forces the author to consider the value they are trying to achieve for the identified role

Sometimes, the user specifies qualities that the outcome has to have to be satisfactory. The User Story mold allows for including non-functional requirements (a.k.a. quality requirements), for instance:

As a trainee (role), I can see all classes that cover topics in which I need training (outcome) within the next six months (quality requirement) so I can plan my career development path (value).

Or using the goal-focused paradigm:

To plan their career development path (value), trainees (role) can see all classes that cover topics in which they need training (outcome) within the next six months (quality requirement).

Another example:

As a loan approver (role), I can view all income and recurring financial obligations the applicant has (outcome) rounded to the nearest dollar (quality requirement) to make a fiscally responsible decision (value).

And:

To make a fiscally responsible decision (value), loan approvers (role) can view all income and recurring financial obligations the applicant has (outcome) rounded to the nearest dollar (quality requirement) .

For simplicity's sake, we are going to forego expressing every User Story in both formats from here on out. We may choose one or the other without indicating a preference for or an advantage one might have over the other.

Lest we forget, the end users of the IT solution are not the only players in the game. There is a wide range of "users" whose perspective you might be missing unless you ask them specifically for their "User Stories".

Here are some examples of User Stories from "non-end" users:

As a business rules administrator, I can modify mortgage conditions to allow the organization to adapt to changing market conditions.

As a webmaster, I can modify the bandwidth to accommodate surges in usage during peak seasons.

As a database administrator, I can recognize when thrashing negatively impacts performance so I can redistribute the tables.

As the CashForecaster System, I need access to the bank's transactions so I can compare my projections to actuals.

This conjures up the question, who (all) should write User Stories? The final example, above, actually indicates that an automated program wrote the User Story. We might someday reach that level of sophisticated software, but in the meantime, the individual responsible for maintaining the CashForecaster System has to represent its interest.

By the way, this example is also an exception and applies only when the story provides incidental or indirect value to a real person. Ideally, someone who plays the role in real life and receives the value has to write the User Story. If people who have not lived the role try to imagine it, the stories lose value rapidly.

Online resources for you:

⇨   A User Story Primer By Dean Leffingwell with Pete Behrens
   http://trailridgeconsulting.com/files/user-story-primer.pdf

It is important to emphasize that a User Story is not a requirement in the traditional meaning of the word. As noted earlier, it is a trigger for a conversation between developers and the representative of the role (often, the "Product Owner").

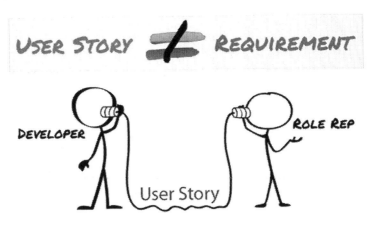

That discussion will take place immediately before developers start to write software to enable that particular story. Postponing the discussion until developers need the knowledge has two major advantages:

1.   When developers start to write the software, the knowledge is fresh in their minds, which means they are less likely to miss something.

2.   No one is spending time elaborating stories that no one will use. User needs change over time. Developers may never have to implement some User Stories, so why waste time delving into excruciating detail about them.

Whereas User Stories are awesome for expressing Stakeholder Requirements, they are not all that the developers need to deliver a working business solution. They do not express the more technology oriented functional solution requirements at an appropriate level of detail. This is why each User Story has a detail level. It is named differently in different methodologies but the same principles apply.

In his book "User Stories Applied: For Agile Software Development", Mike Cohn describes the three parts of a User Story - the Card, the Conversation and the Confirmation. The Card contains the User Story as we described in the preceding pages. Each User Story is written on an index card, PostIt note, or User Story software. User Stories were originally written exclusively on the front side of an index card to support simplicity and brevity. Today you can use specialized User Story software.

When a developer is ready to code a particular User Story, she or he initiates the second C — Conversations. This part of the development process is also referred to as "User Story Elaboration". As the project progresses there will be a number of these conversations.

The final C is Confirmation. These are the Acceptance Criteria for the User story - the details which will enable the customers and the technical team to agree that "if this User Story meets these criteria it is done". The most common format for these acceptance criteria is expressed as "Given-When-Then".

(Given) some context
(When) some action is carried out
(Then) a particular set of observable consequences should obtain

---

Online resources for you:

⇨ Using "Given-When-Then" to Discover and Validate Requirements
https://www.ebgconsulting.com/blog/using-given-when-then-to-discover-and-validate-requirements-2/

There are many different ways to define the Acceptance Criteria of a User Story. This book focuses entirely on how to express the initial User Story (aka the "Card") statement and does not address the "Conversation" or the "Confirmation". Just as a last note, each User Story will have a number of other elements which will help ensure the right software is built - these could include screen mockups, technical notes, process diagrams, data models, and whatever the team needs to enable them to deliver the business value.

In addition, "non-functional" requirements (aka quality requirements) influence how developers implement the User Stories but the stories might not explicitly express them. User story elaboration generally identifies functional and non-functional requirements.

Online resources for you:

⇨ Non-Functional Requirements: Do User Stories Really Help?
http://www.methodsandtools.com/archive/archive.php?id=113

⇨ Nonfunctional Requirements Abstract *(Scaled Agile Framework)*
http://scaledagileframework.com/nonfunctional-requirements/

Finally, since you can only define Transition Requirements once developers design the solution, you may need additional User Stories or other modes to express how to rollout the evolving solution whenever it or a piece of it is ready for prime time.

Given that the primary requirement level that User Stories express is the stakeholder level, the focus of this book is on writing effective User Stories. The next chapters unveil a series of five rules that will make your User Stories more effective. If you apply these rules to your writing, over time they will become automatic allowing you to become more agile in producing them. Given that, let's talk rules.

RULE 1: KEEP YOU USER STORIES SIMPLE

Well-structured User Stories express a single action to achieve a specific goal. Trying to express too much in a User Story adds confusion and increases the amount of discussion needed for developers to understand what the story really means.

Questions answered in this chapter:

- What structure should you use for a User Story?
- How can you limit the need for discussion over the meaning of a User Story?

User Stories are one of the most popular forms for expressing Stakeholder Requirements on projects whether your project follows an Agile approach or a more traditional methodology. Many feel that the mold: As a {role the author represents}, I/we can {do or have something} {with these qualities} to {achieve my goal or objective} by itself is sufficient to explain how to write User Stories. I believe there are still a few dimensions missing.

For instance, examine two implementations of this mold:

As a website visitor (role), I can view all training (do something) which I need (quality requirement) to qualify for the CBAP® exam (goal).

> **As a human being (role), I can differentiate sounds (do something) in my native tongue (quality requirement) to comprehend what others are saying (goal).**

Note that both statements follow the mold and, by that definition, are User Stories. Whereas the first gives the developers great guidance, I question the value of the second. As a result, I have developed a set of guidelines (rules) for writing an effective User Story that go beyond the basic structure and might help you.

The first rule in writing an effective User Story is simple:

Rule 1 for writing an effective user story

K Keep
I It (user story)
S Simple

Online resources for you:

⇨ View this chapter as a video
http://businessanalysisexperts.com/product/keep-your-user-story-simple/

A simple sentence states only one thing. However, it does a good job at that. If you try to express too much in a single sentence, you add confusion. For instance, the User Story,

---

As an applicant, I can navigate to the coverage screen, enter personal and vehicle data, and submit the application online to request automobile insurance coverage.

---

contains 3 distinct thoughts. It would be clearer if you expressed each thought as a single User Story, i.e.,

---

1. **As an applicant, I can navigate to the coverage screen to select insurance coverage I need.**

2. **As an applicant, I can enter personal and vehicle data to compare premiums.**

3. **As an applicant, I can submit an application online to request automobile insurance coverage.**

Compound sentences are, by definition, never simple. That means, you should not have 'if, ands or buts' in the User Story. Well, you actually have to take that with a grain of salt. The word "and" is a phenomenally versatile word in the English language and, in my experience, in any language. It can be a sign of a compound sentence

- if the sentence contains two phrases each of which contains an action (verb) and a subject or object (nouns). The other use of the word "and" is to create a list of items based on common characteristics.

For example, let's look again at our previous example. The original User Story,

---

As an applicant, I can navigate to the coverage screen, enter personal and vehicle data, *and submit the application* (compound sentence) online to request automobile insurance coverage.

---

uses the word "and" in the phrase "and submit the application . . . " to create a compound sentence. The use of "and" in the User Story below, simply connects common types of data.

As an applicant, I can enter *personal and vehicle data* (connecting data) to compare premiums.

I also recommend against using delimiting phrases starting with words like "unless" or "except" in the User Story.

For instance, the User Story:

> As an underwriter, I can override a coverage denial for an applicant to increase our customer base unless **(delimiting phrases)** the denial was due to bad credit in which case I can confirm the denial to protect our customer base.

is confusing and would be much simpler expressed as two User Stories:

1. As an underwriter, I can override a coverage denial for an applicant with good credit to increase our customer base.

2. As an underwriter, I can confirm the coverage denial for an applicant with bad credit to protect our customer base.

Delimiting phrases commonly create a User Story with two different goals. By expressing each goal in a separate User Story, the intent and purpose of each becomes much clearer.

To sum up the first rule,

An effective User Story is a simple sentence that does not contain conjunctions (and, or, but, etc.) or limiting phrases (unless, without, except, etc.).

Following this rule facilitates User Story elaboration, the process whereby developers later ensure they understand the User Story and can implement it.

RULE 2: EXPRESS THE WHAT, NOT THE HOW

When writing User Stories, stakeholders should focus on what they want/need as the business outcome once the User Story has been implemented. Technology decisions should be left up to the developers.

Questions answered in this chapter:

- How can you make sure that your User Story expresses the what and not the how?
- Why is it important that you distinguish between what and how?

What else can you as the author do to make your life and your developers' lives easier? In a word, lots. Rule 2 in the series states, "An effective User Story emphasizes 'what' should be done, not 'how' to do it."

Since the birth of the Information Technology (IT) profession (and presumably even before that), developers (or builders of any kind) have been asking the business community (their customers) to tell them "what" they want, not "how" to develop it. After all, the "how" is really the dominion of the developer community — it is their job. The problem, as always, lies in the detail of how to follow this seemingly simple rule. So let us analyze the "what-not-how" rule to see what it is really all about.

Primarily, it is about focusing on the business results and avoiding thinking about how to achieve them. Avoiding preconceived solutions seems like a great idea, because all too often, your overworked developers will simply implement what you ask for without considering whether it is the best alternative.

WE NEED WINDMILLS

(THIS EXCLUDES OTHER OPTIONS)

You need to avoid what I call "the solution trap", also known as the "how trap". Think about "What" business result you want to achieve and let the developers think about "how" they can achieve it given your parameters. You can do this by thinking about the destination instead of the journey.

Here is a good example:

Let us say I am teaching a class in Houston next Thursday and Friday. The class starts at 8:30 AM Thursday morning. If I were to formulate a User Story in that context, I could say,

As a traveler, I can book a flight leaving the day before the class starts to be on time for the class.

Note that this complies with Rule 1 and the suggested structure for a User Story. However, expressed that way I am limiting my choices. "Booking a flight" is a "how" or expressed differently: "It's a preconceived solution" because it assumes I will fly there.

How about I say:

As a traveler, I can be at the customer site at the designated time on the morning of the first day to begin the class on time.

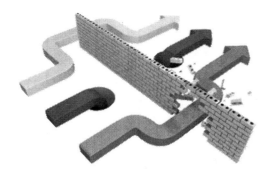

That leaves me with lots of options to fill my business need. I could fly there on Wednesday and stay overnight in a hotel (like most civilized folk would probably do). I could drive there in my motorhome in a couple of days or even hitchhike from my home if I feel lucky and relish the added element of uncertainty.

The point is, there are many possible ways of satisfying the business need, so do not get hung up on the 'obvious' solution too soon. Try to think about business logic or rules instead of technology solutions.

Let us look at a real example to clarify exactly how subtle the difference can be. If a Subject Matter Expert (SME) has a problem with customers entering invalid state abbreviations in the address box of a form, they might be tempted to write the User Story,

---

As an applicant, I can select my state from a drop-down box of abbreviations to avoid entering an invalid state

---

That way, the SME will never get an illegal state abbreviation. The problem is that a drop-down box is actually a specific technology. Not necessarily a bad one, by the way, but not necessarily the best either. If instead of jumping to the solution, the SME considers what she is really trying to achieve, a better User Story might be,

---

As an applicant, I can submit a valid state abbreviation to ensure an accurate quote for insurance coverage.

This expresses WHAT the business needs (a valid state abbreviation) without specifying HOW we are going to achieve that (the drop-down box).

Why is this important? By avoiding premature technology decisions, the User Story actually becomes more valuable. If your User Story tells the developer that you want a drop-down box, he or she may not even consider any other options. Perhaps instead of using a drop-down, it would be possible to automate the process by using the zip code and a web app that returns the state automatically. As a website visitor, I appreciate any solution that reduces or eliminates mistakes I can make.

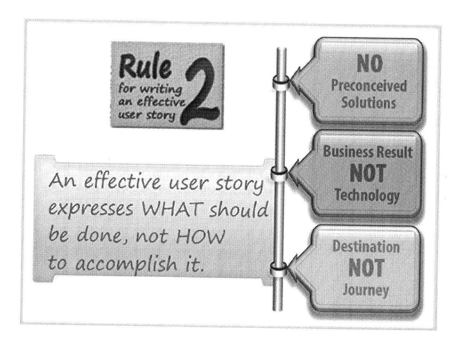

As succinctly as possible, Rule 2 states:

An effective User Story expresses "what" should be done, not "how" to accomplish it by

- ☑ avoiding preconceived solutions

- ☑ describing the business result, not the technology needed, and

- ☑ expressing the destination, not the journey.

If you follow this simple recommendation, your User Stories will be much more effective.

Online resources for you:

⇒   View this chapter as a video
http://businessanalysisexperts.com/product/a-user-story-expresses-
what-not-how/

RULE 3: WRITE RELEVANT USER STORIES

As the author of User Stories, you need to focus on writing stories that the delivered solution will provide. Ensuring that your User Stories are relevant reduces the time wasted writing and elaborating unneeded User Stories.

Questions answered in this chapter:

- How can you decide whether a potential User Story is relevant?
- Why is relevance important?

You are a business professional. Someone has asked you to write User Stories for a planned change to your information technology (IT) application. You now know the first two rules to write effective User Stories", let us recap them here:

1. An effective User Story is a simple sentence that does not contain conjunctions or limiting phrases.

2. An effective User Story emphasizes "what" the solution does, not "how" it does it.

Great, that is how you express an effective User Story, but what about the content? What will make a good User Story?

It is time to discuss Rule 3, namely: "An effective User Story is relevant to (in scope of) the project."

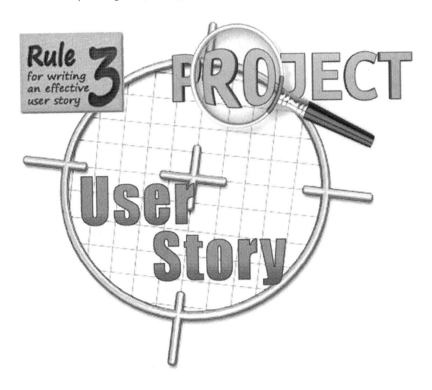

When you sit down to write your User Stories, you need to consider what the project will deliver. In the world of IT, there are a couple of options for delineating what a project can and cannot do. What you are looking for is something called a "Project Charter" or a "Project Scope Statement".

A **Project Charter** typically describes the project in general terms such as:

Policyholders should be able to manage their automobile policies on the web. We need to support web-based policy payments and allow prospects to apply for and be issued temporary proof of insurance coverage pending underwriting rate approval.

Online resources for you:

⇨ Project Charter - Meaning, Importance and its Elements
http://www.managementstudyguide.com/assembling-project-charter.htm

⇨ Six Sigma Project Charter with Template
http://www.isixsigma.com/tools-templates/project-charter/six-sigma-project-charter/

A **Scope statement** is usually much more specific, so it might read more like:

This project will enhance our web-based Policy Maintenance System by allowing policyholders to interact directly with their automobile insurance policies via secure internet access. The web application will allow prospects to request temporary insurance coverage (pending underwriting rate approval), submit payment for outstanding premiums, and update personal and/ or vehicle data. It will not support claims processing.

Online resources for you:

⇨ Example of a project scope statement
http://onlinelibrary.wiley.com/doi/10.1002/9780470432723.app2/pdf

⇨ Writing a Scope Statement
http://www.brighthubpm.com/templates-forms/2491-writing-a-scope-statement/

⇨ How to define the scope of a project
http://www.cio.com.au/article/401353/how_define_scope_project/

As you can see, either delineates your project from the environment of the organization by establishing the boundaries for your project. Whereas the charter can be somewhat vague, the scope statement typically specifies business processes, functions, organizational units, roles or jobs, etc. that the project might affect or influence.

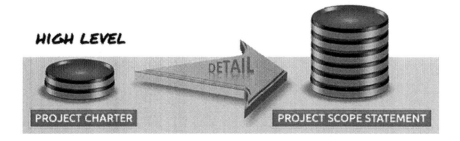

It can also specifically exclude certain components (in our example, claims processing) to further clarify what the project will not do. The User Stories you write have to fit pretty much entirely inside the boundaries that the project charter or scope statement define to be relevant to the project.

In an Agile environment, the Agile team will ask you to elaborate on the story when they are ready to start coding (which could be in a couple of months). In a conventional environment, the business analyst will do the same but before publishing a Business Requirements Document (BRD) — which might be tomorrow.

Online resources for you:

⇨ Introduction to Scrum
  http://scrumtrainingseries.com/Intro_to_Scrum/Intro_to_Scrum.htm

⇨ Sprint Planning Meeting
  http://scrumtrainingseries.com/SprintPlanningMeeting/SprintPlanning Meeting.htm

⇨ Business Requirements Document
  https://www.youtube.com/watch?v=ds8MQPPo1oU

In either case, discovering that your User Story is not in scope for the project at that time is unsettling to say the least. If you express your User Story so it is relevant to the project, you waste less time writing, elaborating, and discarding them. You also avoid bloating the backlog or requirements document with User Stories that the project will not implement which saves considerable time for the entire team. The question is how you can ensure that your User Stories are relevant while you write them.

Relevant User Stories define what the SME (Subject Matter Expert) needs or wants within the project charter or scope statement. Let us put you in the position of being the underwriting SME for this project. As such, your primary duties consist of ensuring that every issued policy poses an acceptable risk as defined by business rules and legal mandates.

You currently underwrite policy changes submitted by insurance agents who have been trained by your organization in submitting insurance applications. Your primary concern for the web-based automobile insurance application is ensuring that policies issued by the website meet the same criteria as those issued by agencies. Following Rules 1 and 2 for writing an effective User Story, you might be tempted to write,

---

As an underwriter, I can underwrite policies from the website to ensure their accuracy and legality.

There, that meets **Rule 1** (simple, well structured) and **Rule 2** (what not how). Is this User Story relevant in its entirety for the boundaries established by the project charter and scope statement?

Asked to elaborate on that User Story, you explain everything you do to underwrite any submitted insurance application. The problem is that you do many things that are not within the scope of the web app and those things are irrelevant from the perspective of this project. For instance, one of the steps you always do is check the claims system to see if the applicant has any existing claims to avoid underwriting a policy to an unqualified person. Since the Scope Statement explicitly excludes claims, that activity is irrelevant to this project.

There are potentially many other steps in your underwriting process that the web app will not affect, but you get the gist. Express your User Story at a level of detail that to the best of your knowledge the project can deliver.

For example, you might write,

As an underwriter, I can check the applicant's submitted driver's license data with the issuing state authority to confirm age, gender, and place of residence.

Another example,

As an underwriter, I can evaluate an applicant's driving record to confirm that the applicant qualifies for the selected coverage rates.

Either of these relates specifically to data that the web app has to deliver so you can do your job. A more difficult to quantify aspect of a User Story is it's "tail". The tail of the User Story encompasses the consequences of implementing it.

A good example is the User Story

To comply with legal requirements, underwriters can report vehicles removed from a policy to the respective state's Department of Motor Vehicles (DMV) .

There is potential fallout from implementing this User Story. Assume that the law requires us to notify the respective state's Department of Motor Vehicles that the previously insured vehicle is no longer covered. Who within the organization has the authority to formulate and send this notice? If it is the underwriting department, perhaps the Change Vehicle User Story is relevant as written. If an external department (e.g., Legal or Regulatory) is responsible, you can express this User Story better as

---

To send notice to the respective DMV, underwriters can report vehicles removed from a policy to the Legal Department.

This assumes that Legal should not notify the DMV to remove the vehicle until you have underwritten the change. Consider whether your User Story could cause a cascading change that exceeds the project charter or scope and revise it to be in scope.

To summarize, the third rule of effective User Stories reads:

An effective User Story targets components that are relevant to the project in that it:

☑   Falls within the project charter or scope statement;

☑   Defines something about the solution that the business community needs or wants; and

☑   Has a short "tail" (does not create a cascading effect of changes that exceed the project's authority).

Keeping your User Story relevant will save you and the project time and money and make you much more popular with the IT department – and who knows where that could lead.

Online resources for you:

⇨ View this chapter as a video
http://businessanalysisexperts.com/product/writing-user-stories-in-scope/

RULE 4: AVOID AMBIGUITY IN A USER STORY

Ambiguity is communication's biggest threat. If your User Story contains ambiguous words or phrases, the solution may not be what you desire.

Questions answered in this chapter:

- How can you ensure that your audience understands your User Story as you intend it?
- How does ambiguity affect the quality of the solution?

In the world of information technology, developers often do not know until their product is finished whether or not it is what the customer wanted. Misunderstood, ambiguous, and assumption-laden statements cause more project failures than any other single factor.

I SAW HER DUCK

Study after study confirms that simple fact. Unless all participants involved in the process of planning, designing, developing, validating and delivering the technology share a common understanding of what they are doing, your projects are at high risk of failure.

The major obstacle to effective communication is ambiguity, meaning using terms and phrases that different members of your target audience will interpret differently. If your project is using an Agile software development approach the project team will address ambiguity conversationally during the elaboration of the User Story. However, even in an agile scenario it can be beneficial to remove ambiguity earlier, for example, before you add the User Story to the backlog to facilitate Sprint planning.

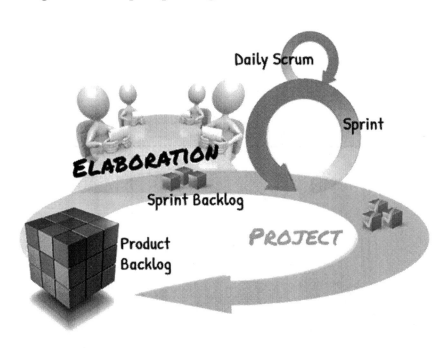

In Waterfall and Iterative development approaches it is much more important to remove ambiguity in the early analysis phases. The less ambiguity you have in the phrasing of a User Story at the beginning, the more likely it is that the solution will deliver what you want with minimal cost.

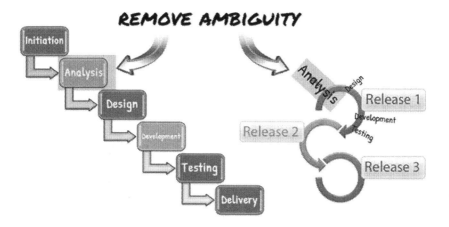

Online resources for you:

⇨ Business Analysis and System Development Methodologies
http://businessanalysisexperts.com/product/business-analysis-sdm-system-development-methodologies/

⇨ Business Analysis and Agile Methodologies
http://businessanalysisexperts.com/product/business-analysis-agile-methodologies/

⇨ Business Analysis and Waterfall Methodologies
http://businessanalysisexperts.com/product/business-analyst-waterfall-methodologies/

⇨ Business Analysis and Iterative Methodologies
http://businessanalysisexperts.com/product/business-analysis-iterative-methodologies/

What causes ambiguity in the first place? As the author of the User Story, you know what the User Story means. It seems so simple, you would think that the rest of the world should "get it" right away. For instance, assume you are the manager of inventory acquisition in an organization. Your job is to purchase enough of each product to be able to meet future customer demands but not have more than is necessary to avoid tying up too much capital in inventory. When someone asks you what you want your future Automated Product Replenishment (APR) system to do, you might simply say something like, "Well, for starters, we need a forecast".

If you follow the first 3 rules for writing effective User Stories, you would have written

---

As Manager of Inventory Acquisition,
I can order the correct amount of product we will sell
to avoid tying up too much capital in inventory.

This statement meets the first three rules, it

1. is a simple sentence that does not contain conjunctions or limiting phrases,

2. emphasizes "what" the solution does, not "how" it does it, and

3. targets components that are relevant to the project.

So what could possibly be unclear about that statement? The first thing we need to do is to identify words or phrases that might be ambiguous or easily misunderstood. Revisit your simple, complete, well-structured User Story for a minute to see if there is anything ambiguous.

What about the phrase "correct amount"?

As Manager of Inventory Acquisition,
I can order the **correct amount** of product we will sell
to avoid tying up too much capital in inventory.

Who determines what the correct amount is? How do you measure the "amount", individual items, cases, palettes, truckloads, or something else entirely?

As Manager of Inventory Acquisition, I can order the
correct amount of product **we will sell** to avoid tying up
too much capital in inventory.

When you write, "we will sell", do you have a specific timespan in mind, meaning within the next day, week, month, year, or until the company goes out of business? How much capital is "too much capital"? How exactly do you calculate how much capital is "tied up in inventory"?

Online resources for you:

⇨ Taming Ambiguity in Natural Language Requirements
http://prof.kamsties.com/download/icssea2000.pdf

⇨ Collection of Ambiguous or Inconsistent/Incomplete
Statements
http://www.gray-area.org/Research/Ambig/

As you can see, although this simple, complete and well-structured sentence seems very good, it still has a lot of potential ambiguity. However, you know what you meant when you wrote the User Story, so it is difficult for you to identify ambiguous phrases. You have to switch hats. You need to **"be the reader, not the author"**.

To get started, simply read your User Stories and try your best to misunderstand them. To get the biggest effect from this exercise, we recommend performing the critical review in a different environment than the one in which you wrote the statements. For instance, if you wrote the User Stories in the morning, review them in the afternoon (or vice versa). If you wrote them at your desk, review them at home or on your commute. By changing the time or the physical environment, you might change your perception of what you wrote. We call this activity "desk checking" and you might be amazed at how much ambiguity you can identify when you really focus on it.

Once you have completed desk checking, you might think that you have unambiguous User Stories, but what do others think? Since the User Story is a fundamental tool of communication between the business community and the IT team (and forms the foundation of a future IT solution), you might want to run it by a colleague, a peer, or your manager to get their take on it.

One of the best ways to test whether or not someone else truly understands a User Story **the way you intended** is by asking him or her to rewrite it - **and not use any of your words** except for simple articles ("a", "an", "the", etc.), prepositions, pronouns, and conjunctions. Specifically, the other person cannot use any of your nouns, verbs, adverbs or adjectives (the "meat" of the User Story).

This little exercise actually forces the other person to think outside the box. It forces him or her to use terms that are different but mean the same thing to them. If you can read their User Story and you both agree that it still means the same as your original User Story, you can feel a lot more confident that you are getting your point across. If, however, you have to ask them why they used a specific word that means something different than you intended, that should be a red flag. Consider revising your User Story to make sure that the two of you agree on a common meaning.

Let us look at a real-life example.

As a telephone operator, I can complete at least 12 reservations per hour during peak volume to reduce the wait times for customers.

This looks like a reasonable User Story in the context of a call center for a travel agency. I gave this to a colleague and asked her to rewrite it following our rules. Her rewrite came back,

---

As a reservationist, I am able to process a minimum of a dozen requests for travel accommodations within 60 minutes during the busiest time of the year to minimize dropped calls.

Fascinating; what value does her rewrite give me? Switching the role from my "telephone operator" to "reservationist" actually makes me reconsider what role should write the User Story. The term "telephone operator" is generic. It describes my job whereas the "reservationist" actually better describes the role in this particular User Story. She also changed my "can complete" to "am able to process". I have an aversion to the verb "process" because it is a poster child for ambiguity, so in the end we agreed that "can complete" is the best option. Changing "12" to "a dozen" added nothing and the word "reservations" is a standard term in the travel industry, so we stuck with it.

Her translation of "at least" into "a minimum of" did not seem relevant at first. However, when we discussed the phrases "peak volume" and "the busiest time of the year", things changed. When I wrote the original story, I was thinking about peak times of the day without considering seasonal influences. The times leading up to major holidays tend to be extremely busy and holiday travel plans tend to get more complicated. Those reservations often involve whole families and considerable effort in identifying the cheapest alternatives, so they tend to take longer. During those times, it could become impossible to achieve my goal – I had to rephrase it.

In addition, her translation of my "reduce the wait times for customers" to "minimize dropped calls" really got my attention because overly long wait times actually cause the majority of dropped calls. Her rewrite forced me to contemplate what the real business benefit that I expected from this User Story was. In the end, I decided to revise my original statement to read,

---

As a reservationist, I can complete at least 12 non-holiday reservations per hour during daily peak times to reduce dropped calls caused by long wait times.

You can see from the example that the simple act of analyzing the way someone else interpreted my original User Story was very revealing indeed. It gave me an insight into their thinking and could have potentially averted a costly miscommunication farther down the line. If you are going to try this little technique, two words of advice.

Due to the physical structure of our brains, different genders often think differently. You will get better feedback if you pick someone from the opposite sex to interpret your sentence.

Online resources for you:

⇨ Brain Sex: The Real Difference Between Men and Women
   http://www.amazon.com/Brain-Sex-Difference-Between-Women/dp/0385311834

⇨ Girl Brain, Boy Brain?
   http://www.scientificamerican.com/article/girl-brain-boy-brain/

⇨ Differences between males' and females' brains
   https://www.youtube.com/watch?v=vKVwcwXc4Dk

In addition, different job functions require different thinking styles, so you might ask a developer or designer (someone who will later actually have to understand the sentence) to do the rewrite. Following these two recommendations should drastically improve the quality of your feedback and the entire process of assessing the ambiguity in your User Story will definitely improve the quality of the delivered solution.

Succinctly put, Rule 4 states:

An effective User Story is

☑ easily understandable,

☑ unambiguous, and

☑ clear to all target audiences.

Removing ambiguity is definitely a first step toward improving communication between those who want a solution and those who deliver it.

Online resources for you:

⇨ View this chapter as a video
  http://businessanalysisexperts.com/product/avoid-ambiguity-user-story/

RULE 5: DEVELOP MEASURABLE NON-FUNCTIONAL REQUIREMENTS

> Non-functional requirements are your best weapon in the war against unsatisfactory performance in IT solutions. Whether you use User Stories or conventional requirements, non-functional requirements are king.

Questions answered in this chapter:

- How do you express non-functional (quality) requirements?
- What value do non-functional requirements add to your User Stories?

I would like to start this chapter with a story that has nothing to do with information technology. It is, however, extremely relevant to the process of expressing User Stories in measurable terms.

I was out to dinner a while back with a couple of my friends at a restaurant that one friend in particular, (Brad) frequented. Brad was a huge fan of buffalo wings, but he only enjoyed them when they were extremely well done (in his opinion – I would consider them totally ruined)! He often ate at this particular restaurant and expected that they would know how he liked his wings. He ordered them very well done and added, "You know how I like them." When his order arrived, the wings were, of course, not even close to well done by his standards. He sent them back and instructed the server to tell the chef to "make them really, really crispy" to make sure that they would be done well enough. The delivered wings were slightly darker, but still not to his liking.

Brad sent his wings back 3 more times(!), politely requesting that they "over cook", "sear", and "burn the suckers" in attempts to get the meal he wanted. After the fifth time, the wings (although still not entirely to Brad's satisfaction) were at least edible.

When the restaurant manager showed up to ask if everything was all right, he got the full story. Irritated, he went back to the kitchen to speak with the chef. When he returned, he explained to Brad that they had "deep-fried the wings 12 minutes at the prescribed temperature of 375°F which was excessive by the chef's standards" and that if he wanted them even more done in the future he should order his wings "deep-fried for 17 minutes".

On his next visit to this restaurant, my friend complied and (after assuring the server three times that he knew exactly what he wanted), finally enjoyed his wings deep-fried to his satisfaction right away.

The moral of this story, of course, is that it is not enough to know what you want. You need to be able to specify in measurable terms how a third party (in this case the chef; in the world of IT, the developers) can deliver what you want.

The latest possible time when you have to define the measurable dimensions is immediately before the developers start coding. You should prepare yourself, however, by thinking of this in advance. If your non-functional requirements are not objectively measurable, you need to revise, rewrite, or expand them.

Online resources for you:

⇨ Common Requirements Problems, Their Negative Consequences, and the Industry Best Practices to Help Solve Them
http://www.jot.fm/issues/issue_2007_01/column2.pdf

User stories take a dramatically different approach to solving the age-old problem of communication between developers and the user community and that difference has a significant impact on measurability. If you follow the User Story paradigm faithfully, you captured your User Story on the front of a 3X5" index card. If you use any other tool to capture it, you should still attempt to constrain the length of the User Story to one or two brief sentences. Remember our example,

As a call center operator, I can complete at least 12 reservations per hour during peak traffic to minimize wait times for customers.

or expressed in the goal-focused structure,

To minimize wait times for customers, each call center operator can complete at least 12 reservations per hour during peak traffic.

Following the User Story paradigm, developers are not concerned with any additional details about the User Story until they initiate the development process for the selected User Story. At that time, they should schedule some time with you as the author of the User Story to delve in to the nitty-gritty details. During this discussion, the developer will jot down on the back of the index card (or in the appropriate tool) how they can prove that their solution meets your needs once they deliver it. If the measurable quality of the User Story is expressed in specific numbers, the discussion can focus on why that particular number is important, how much leeway if any there is in the number, and possibly how exactly the quality will be counted. Some legitimate questions for our example might be:

⇨ What defines a "completed reservation?

⇨ How will we treat reservations that are incomplete,

⇨ as in the caller decides not to accept the offer?

⇨ What constitutes 'peak traffic'?

⇨ What are the expectations during 'non-peak traffic'?

⇨ What makes the number 12 so important?

Obviously, developers could simply accept the statement as expressed (or more correctly, as they interpret it) and implement it with impunity, but if they challenge the statement before development starts, it might change and there is no cheaper time to change than now (prior to coding).

Online resources for you:

⇨ How do you get more out of your User Stories?
   http://www.slideshare.net/ThoughtWorks/gettingmoreoutofuserstorie s-130405024009phpapp01

⇨ Agile in Practice Help Sheet Story Cards
   http://www.agileacademy.com.au/agile/sites/default/files/Story%20Ca rds%202011.pdf

---

To return to our example with Brad, he could use the User Story format to order his wings:

As a diner, I want my buffalo wings deep-fried at the standard temperature for 17 minutes which I consider to be well-done.

Assuming the chef followed his instructions and could (if need be) prove to Brad that he deep-fried the wings at the 375°F (the standard temperature for deep-frying chicken wings) for exactly 17 minutes, there could no longer be a debate about whether the meal met Brad's specification. Even if the wings came out black as charcoal (the way Brad really loved them!), that would not be the chef's problem.

If the chef thought these instructions would pose a danger to Brad, he should rightfully challenge the request, but if Brad accepted responsibility for the outcome, the request should be honored.

Measurable qualities define acceptable behavior for the system from the user perspective. The challenge is that there are two categories of "measurable" qualities, objective and subjective measures.

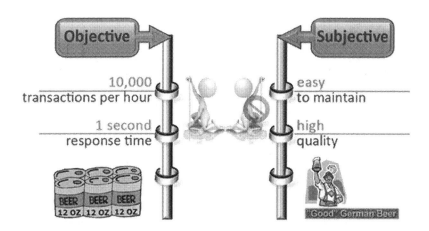

Measurable qualities containing numbers (as in, "10,000 transactions per hour", or "one second response time", or as our example shows, simply "a 6-pack") can be objectively measured and validated by a third party. Subjective qualities (like, "easy to maintain", "high quality", or - if you are a beer drinker - "good beer") by definition cannot be objectively measured. These qualities are valid performance needs from the business perspective but to be usable in a User Story, you need to clarify them. To deliver a solution that meets your needs, developers need qualities (a.k.a. non-functional requirements) expressed in measurable terms. What are some of the non-functional requirements that you as the author of a User Story need to define?

- ☑ **Frequency** – how often do people playing the identified role need this User Story?

- ☑ **Urgency** – how quickly does the application have to respond to a user's needs?

- ☑ **Volume** – how much business data will the application maintain for this User Story?

- ☑ **Accuracy** – how precise and timely does the data have to be from a business perspective?

- ☑ **Usability** – what features make the application easily usable by the role?

- ☑ **Learnability** – how quickly can new users in this role learn how to use the application?

- ☑ **Flexibility / Scalability** – how fast do you anticipate frequency and volume to change?

- ☑ **Reliability** – how critical is it that the application does not fail?

These are examples of **non-functional requirements** that you might need to define whether you use User Story or any other form to express your requirements. The key point is that the business community needs to define these from the business perspective before the project moves into the development or purchasing phase. The technology exists to achieve almost any goal you can think of assuming that you can afford it. Only if the business community defines the goal in measurable terms in advance do they have a legitimate right to expect that the delivered solution will meet their needs.

Online resources for you:

⇨ Non-functional Requirements *(Scaled Agile Framework)*
   http://scaledagileframework.com/nonfunctional-requirements/

⇨ Non-Functional Requirements *(University of Texas at Dallas)*
   http://www.utd.edu/~chung/RE/NFR-18-4-on-1.pdf

⇨ Types of Non-functional Requirements
   https://www.youtube.com/watch?v=AjLWQg6jGIA

The question is not whether you need to specify measurable qualities in your User Stories, but rather who is responsible for them, the business community, the business analyst, or the developer community?

The correct answer is all three!

Developers are obviously involved in getting the technology to work fast enough to meet the highest expected traffic, but it is the business community's job to anticipate just how high that is. The one wearing the business analysis hat is responsible for capturing, clarifying, and confirming User Stories. That individual has to make the business community aware of the issues and ask the tough questions.

In summary, Rule 5 states that an effective User Story is expressed in objectively measurable terms.

Assuming that non-functional requirements will take care of themselves has proven to be a high-risk endeavor for many organizations.

Online resources for you:

⇨ View this chapter as a video
  http://businessanalysisexperts.com/product/non-functional-requirements-user-stories/

SUMMARY

Remember, the fundamental purpose of a User Story is to express a business need from the perspective of a specified role and explain the business value that role desires. Follow these simple rules in writing your User Stories to express what you want and why. They will improve the odds that you actually get what you want.

On the next page, we provide a simple job aid that summarizes the **5 rules** for posting them on your bulletin board or pin to your cubicle wall.

An Effective User Story ...

1) ... **is a simple sentence** that does not contain conjunctions (and, or, but, etc.) or limiting phrases (unless, without, except, etc.);

2) ... **expresses "what" should be done, not "how"** to accomplish it by:

   a) avoiding preconceived solutions,

   b) describing the business result, not the technology needed, and

   c) expressing the destination, not the journey;

3) ... **targets components that are relevant** to the project in that it:

   a) falls within the project charter or scope statement,

   b) defines something about the solution that the business community needs or wants, and

   c) has a short "tail" (does not create a cascading effect of changes that exceed the project's authority);

4) ... **is easily understandable, unambiguous, and clear** to all target audiences; and

5) ... **is objectively measurable** so it can be validated by an independent third party.

Just be prepared to explain to the developers how you will prove that your User Story is met when they ask.

ABOUT THE AUTHORS

Angela and Tom Hathaway have authored and delivered hundreds of training courses and publications for business analysts around the world. They have facilitated hundreds of requirements discovery sessions for information technology projects under a variety of acronyms (JAD, ASAP, JADr, JRP, etc.).

Based on their personal journey and experiences reported by their students, they recognized how much anyone can benefit from a basic understanding of what is currently called "business analysis". Their mission is to allow everyone, anywhere access to simple, easy-to-learn techniques by sharing their experience and expertise in their training seminars, blogs, books, and public presentations.

At BA-EXPERTS (http://businessanalysisexperts.com/) we focus exclusively on Business Analysis for **"anyone wearing the BA hat™"**. We believe that business analysis has become a needed skill for every business professional whether or not they have the title Business Analyst. We have made it our goal to enable anyone wearing the BA hat™ to have access to high quality training material and performance support. Please call us at 702-637-4573, email us (Tom.Hathaway@ba-experts.com), or visit our Business Analyst Learning Store at (http://businessanalysisexperts.com/) if you are interested in other training offers.